Nadeem Lutfullah

55 UNCONVENTIONAL INTERVIEW QUESTIONS

Not your usual *'Why should we hire you?'* questions.

Don't stumble over new-generation behavioral questions, developed by recruiters to throw your prep out the window!

Copyright © 2024 Nadeem Shafkat Lutfullah

Nadeem Shafkat Lutfullah asserts the moral right to be identified as the author of this work. All rights reserved. No part of this publication may be reproduced, stored in a retrieval system, or transmitted in any form or by any means—electronic, mechanical, photocopying, recording or otherwise—without prior written permission from the author.

Unauthorized actions relating to this publication may result in civil liability and damages.

Title: *55 Unconventional Interview Questions*
Print Edition ISBN: 978-969-54-9214-7
First Edition: 2024
Cover Design by: Olinart
Published by: Self-published
Website: www.thecareerceo.com

For information on bulk purchases, please visit Amazon.com.

Dedication

To my parents, Shafkat Ahmed Lutfullah and Yasmeen Shafkat, whose unwavering strength, boundless wisdom and selfless dedication have shaped not just lives but legacies. You raised us with honor, unwavering affection, dignity, and an enduring spirit that transcends generations. For everything you gave to your six children, and for everything that you shall ever remain for us, this is for you.

Table of Contents

Preface 1
    What does this mean for you, the job seeker? 1

1. The Evolution of Interview Formats. The New Language of Interviews: Redefining the Playing Field 5
    The Socratic Method. 6

2. Shaping the New Vocabulary: Key Terms and Concepts 11
    The difference between 'making' and 'taking' a decision! 13

3. Shifting From Conventional to Creative: Why Innovation Matters 17

4. The Illusion of Simplicity: Deceptively Easy Questions 21

5. The Creativity Quotient 25
    Emotional intelligence: the human element in interviews. 27
    DRAWING CONCLUSIONS FROM CONTEXT. 29
    Recognizing the pivotal role of context in shaping our understanding of interview questions. 29
    Contextual clues: uncovering hidden meanings. 30
    Phrasing and tone. 30
    Situational context 31
    Non-verbal cues – reading between the lines. 32
    Previous questions – connecting the dots 34
    Tips and warnings 35

Silent signals – what are YOU saying without words?.. 35
The power of pauses – using silence strategically. . 36

THE 55 UNCONVENTIONAL QUESTIONS AND ANSWERS 38-99

Conclusion.. 100

About the Author 102

Preface

As you submit your job applications, a sense of accomplishment mixes with the anticipation of what comes next: the interview.

The prospect of an interview can be both exhilarating and intimidating. The stakes are high, and the outcome can have a significant impact not only on your career future but also on your current mindset.

Beyond the changes brought by the 'new normal' work environment, the recruitment sphere has transformed dramatically post-pandemic, which has also impacted the art of interviewing and how interviews are conducted. Recruiters no longer rely on generic, oft-repeated questions. Today, the savviest of recruiters and hiring managers are employing innovative, unconventional methods and processes to separate the wheat from the chaff, to identify the true gems amidst the ocean of qualified applicants.

What does this mean for you, the job seeker?
Will it be enough to take the traditional route of memorizing

and rehearsing answers to frequently encountered interview questions?

Without a doubt, the answer is a simple 'no'!

You need to be prepared to think on your feet, to respond with agility and wit, and to demonstrate your ability to adapt to the unexpected. Simply put, you need to be able to navigate the surprising twists of interviews with confidence and aplomb.

That's where this book comes in: a comprehensive guide to 55 unconventional interview questions and their answers, designed to push you out of your comfort zone and test your mettle. These questions are not meant to be easy; they are crafted to challenge your thought process, to probe your agility, and to assess your ability to think critically and creatively. They are the questions that will separate the exceptional from the ordinary, the ones that will make you stand out and demonstrate your value as a candidate.

Each answer is crafted to make a strong, lasting impression on the panel. Some of you, depending on your experience level and the industry you belong to, might find the answers too brief. However, my objective in offering you the insights into these novel questions and their answers is to provide you with the thought-foundation to expand and build upon.

In a distinctive feature that sets this book apart, I've introduced the concepts of **'Motive'** and **'Impact'** for each of the 55 questions and their answers. These insights offer you a deeper understanding of the underlying purpose of each question, and the intended effect their responses should have on the interview's outcome.

This unique framework gives candidates a competitive edge, enabling them to not only craft thoughtful answers, but also to grasp how their responses can resonate with interviewers.

To set the stage for this exploration, the book begins with a brief historical journey, tracing the evolution of the interview process from its early origins to the present day, revealing the intricate shifts in interviewing practices and philosophies. Such an approach is rare in interview preparation literature, making this book an invaluable guide to standing out during the hiring process.

Moreover, this book is not just for job seekers or candidates preparing to face an interview; it's an equally valuable resource for H.R. personnel and recruiters, who are looking to stay ahead of the curve and develop innovative new questions, which will give them a deeper insight into a candidate's abilities.

As you progress through this book, you will encounter questions that will challenge your assumptions, questions that will make you think, and questions that will push the limits of your creativity. You'll encounter scenarios that will test your problem-solving skills, your ability to work under pressure and your capacity to think outside the box.

And, through it all, you will emerge stronger, more confident, and capable of tackling the demands of the modern workplace.

So, are you ready to take the leap, to transform how you approach job interviews, and to secure the positions you've always dreamed of? Are you ready to unlock the next level of your career and achieve the success you've always envisioned? Then let us begin this journey together – one that will propel you to the forefront of interview preparation and beyond.

Turn the page and let's get started.

1.
The Evolution of Interview Formats
The New Language of Interviews:
Redefining the Playing Field

It might come as a surprise to many that the evolution of interview formats is a fascinating story which spans centuries, with roots tracing back to ancient civilizations. Understanding this historical background is good knowledge for grasping the significance of modern interview practices, and their role in shaping the whole recruitment cycle.

In the opening sections of this book, we shall explore the shifting dynamics of job interviews, from rigid, formulaic interactions to dynamic conversations that gauge intellect, creativity and cultural fit. We will dissect how the traditional approach has been upended, and how you can harness these changes to your professional advantage.

The earliest recorded forms of job interviews date back to ancient Greece and Rome, where candidates were assessed through a series of oral examinations, debates and, sometimes, a show of physical prowess. These early interview formats were designed to evaluate a candidate's knowledge, eloquence and resilience in standing up to challenges.

The Socratic Method.

The Socratic Method is a form of philosophical inquiry and dialogue developed by the ancient Greek philosopher Socrates. It involved asking and answering questions, to stimulate critical thinking and illuminate ideas.

There are two key aspects of this method that I would like to discuss in relation to their relevance here:

- *Dialogue-based:* the method is characterized by a conversational approach, where questions are posed to stimulate discussion and uncover underlying assumptions.
- *Questioning assumptions:* The Socratic Method focuses on questioning the validity and logic of assumptions and beliefs, rather than simply seeking definitive answers.

In essence, the Socratic Method seeks to foster a deeper

understanding through inquiry and dialogue, making it a powerful tool for exploring complex ideas and challenging preconceived notions.

Fast-forward to the Industrial Revolution, and the interview process began to take on a more formalized structure. With the rise of mass production and the need for a skilled workforce, companies began to develop standardized interview questions and evaluation criteria. This marked the beginning of the 'traditional' interview format, characterized by a rigid, formulaic approach to assessing candidates.

This shift was further accelerated by the rise of globalization, which brought with it a diverse pool of candidates from diverse cultural backgrounds. In the 1980s through to the '90s, the interview format underwent a significant transformation, with the emergence of behavioral interviewing. This approach focused on assessing a candidate's past experiences and behaviors as a predictor of future performance.

The *'STAR'* method, developed by psychologists, became a widely adopted framework for structuring behavioral interview questions.

The 21st century has seen the rise of innovative interview formats, driven in part by technological advancements and the need for companies to stay competitive in a rapidly changing job market. In the past few decades, recruiters and hiring managers started employing unconventional methods – like group assessments and role-plays – to assess certain basic skills, like ease of communication, the candidates' dexterity, and creativity. In recent years, the trend shifted toward more holistic assessments, focusing on a candidate's problem-solving skills, emotional intelligence and cultural fit.

Companies are recognizing that traditional questions and evaluation criteria are no longer sufficient to identify the right people that they seek. Instead, they're seeking candidates who can think critically, adapt to changing circumstances and demonstrate a deep understanding of the roles' challenges, as well as the company's values and mission.

One of the most significant challenges facing recruiters and organizations today is balancing innovation with tradition. While it's essential to stay ahead of the curve by adopting new interview formats, it's equally important to ensure that these approaches remain fair, unbiased and effective in identifying the most suitable potential employees, all while retaining a humanistic touch.

Recognizing the fact that the interview process is not a one-way street is key to mastering it effectively. It's a dynamic conversation between the candidate and the recruiter, with both parties seeking to gain a deeper understanding of each other.

By adopting a holistic approach to interviewing, companies can move beyond mere skills assessment and evaluate a candidate's potential to drive business growth, innovate and thrive in a rapidly changing environment. In other words, companies now seek to hire people who can deliver beyond their expected daily tasks and assignments.

By understanding the historical trajectory of interview formats, we can better appreciate the significance of modern innovations and their role in shaping the recruitment framework.

As you turn the pages of this book, you will delve into the world of unconventional interview questions, exploring the techniques and mindset needed to succeed. I continue to emphasize understanding the interviewer's psyche, rather than simply focusing on how you, as a candidate, should respond to the questions.

2.
Shaping the New Vocabulary: Key Terms and Concepts

Venturing into the world of contemporary interviews, it is essential to grasp the fundamental terms and concepts that underpin modern recruitment strategies.

In this section, we will explore the vocabulary that shapes the interview structure, demystifying terms like *'behavioral and situational questions'*, *'situational judgment tests'*, *'cultural fit'* and *'emotional intelligence'*. These concepts will serve as the foundation for our exploration of the interview process, guiding our discussion and illuminating the intricacies of modern recruitment.

But why is it crucial to understand these terms? The answer lies in the fact that they hold the power to make or break a candidate's chances of success. By grasping the nuances of these concepts, you will be in a stronger position to navigate the interview process, showcasing your skills, creativity, adaptability and problem-solving abilities in the most compelling manner.

Let's begin with the concept of *'behavioral and situational questions'*, where you might be asked to describe particular instances, rather than talking about how you would behave generally. These questions seek to explore a candidate's past experiences, in a bid to understand how they handled challenging situations, and what were the most prominent behavioral traits or characteristics in their reaction to them. Additionally, these questions offer a glimpse into the candidate's inherent tendencies, revealing whether they are more likely to take a reactive stance or a proactive approach when faced with different situations and scenarios.

To prepare for behavioral questions, it is essential to have a clear understanding of the role requirements, and the essential skills needed for the position you are being interviewed for. You may start by making a list of your past experiences, focusing on situations where you demonstrated the desired skills.

Practice answering questions using the 'CAR'[1] *(Context/Action/Results)* method, which involves describing the context of the situation or the incident, and the actions

---

[1] My YouTube video explains the CAR technique in detail: https://youtu.be/6cHoOMHTTtY

taken by you, then rounding up the answer by highlighting the outcomes or the end result of the situation in question.

Next, let's explore the concept of *'situational judgment tests'*, or *'SJTs'*.

These are assessments that present candidates with hypothetical scenarios, asking them to choose the most appropriate course of action. But what's the logic behind the SJTs?

SJTs are essentially designed to evaluate a candidate's decision-making, adaptability and problem-solving skills. Instead of asking the candidates to narrate a scenario, the interviewer presents the candidate with realistic scenarios to evaluate their thought-processes, values and attitudes. These questions are particularly useful in high-stakes roles, such as leadership positions, where the ability to make sound judgments is critical.

The difference between 'making' and 'taking' a decision!
When it comes to decisions, the distinction between making and taking is profound, yet often overlooked. To make a decision implies ownership, initiative and the power to shape an outcome. It's a proactive process, driven by

insight, strategy and a clear vision of the future. In contrast, to *take* a decision suggests acceptance—acting on what is presented, rather than shaping the possibilities yourself. True leaders and innovators don't just take decisions handed to them, they actively make decisions, wielding influence and purpose to drive forward meaningful change.

Another crucial concept in modern interview terminology is *'cultural fit'*.

In job interview terminology, a cultural fit refers to the alignment between a candidate's values, beliefs and attitudes with those of the organization. It's about finding candidates who share the company's vision, mission and values, and who are passionate about contributing to its success. During recent years, this context has expanded to emphasize the growing importance of diversity and inclusion, which are now woven into every facet of recruitment, reflecting a collective shift toward more equitable, representative and culturally enriched workplaces.

Cultural fit is critical in today's competitive job market, where companies are seeking candidates who can drive business growth, innovate, and be trusted to uphold the company's reputation under all circumstances.

To effectively showcase your cultural fit, you must have a clear understanding of the company's values, mission and work environment. Investing time in researching the company's policies, priorities and recent successes or growth can significantly enhance your responses, if you encounter such questions during the interview.

'Emotional intelligence', or *'E.I.Q.' (Emotional Intelligence Quotient)*, refers to the ability to recognize and understand emotions in oneself and others, using this awareness to guide thought and behavior. It's about developing self-awareness, empathy and social skills, enabling you to maneuver complex social situations with ease. E.I. is critical in modern recruitment strategies, as it's a key predictor of job performance, leadership potential and overall success.

To develop your E.I., you need to practice introspection or self-reflection, seeking to understand your emotions, strengths and weaknesses. To improve upon your active listening skills, focus on the needs and expectations of others, seeking to understand the perspectives and feelings of those around you. This will help you develop a deeper understanding of yourself and others, enabling you to better manage the complexities of answering E.I.-based questions at the interview.

3.
Shifting From Conventional to Creative: Why Innovation Matters

Talking about the world of modern interview techniques and methodologies, let us examine a case study that exemplifies the shift from conventional to creative interview questioning.

As a brief case study, our focus will be on Google, a pioneering tech giant that has consistently pushed the boundaries of innovation in recruitment strategies. In the early 2000s, Google was facing a unique challenge: the company was growing at an exponential rate, and its recruitment team was struggling to identify top talent who could keep pace with its rapid expansion. The traditional interview questions, which focused on technical skills and qualifications, were no longer sufficient to evaluate a candidate's potential to thrive in Google's fast-paced and dynamic environment.

Enter Laszlo Bock, Google's former Senior Vice President of People Operations. Bock was determined to revolutionize the interview process, by introducing innovative questions that could assess a candidate's creativity, problem-solving skills and intellectual agility. He believed that these qualities were essential for success in Google's fast-growing collaborative and adaptive work environment.

To address this challenge, Bock and his team developed a range of creative interview questions, which were designed to test a candidate's ability to think outside the box. These questions were often unrelated to the job description, but they provided valuable insights into a candidate's thought processes, values and attitudes. For example, one famous Google interview question was: "How many golf balls can fit in a school bus?" This question was not focused on finding the right answer; instead, it aimed to assess the candidates' cognitive process, and their capacity to think innovatively when under stress.

The results of this groundbreaking method were extraordinary. Google's recruitment team was able to identify top talent, who possessed the skills, creativity and adaptability required to thrive in the company's dynamic environment. The company's growth rate accelerated, and its reputation as a hub for innovation and creativity was cemented.

What can we learn from this case study? Firstly, it highlights the importance of moving beyond traditional interview questions that focus solely on technical skills and qualifications. By introducing creative questions that test a candidate's intellectual agility, companies can gain a more comprehensive understanding of their potential to drive business growth and innovation.

Secondly, this case study demonstrates the value of adopting a holistic approach to interviewing, one that evaluates a candidate's fit with the company's culture, values and mission. By doing so, companies can identify exceptionally talented candidates, who are not only skilled but also passionate about contributing to the organization's success. And, finally, this case study underscores the need for companies to stay ahead of the curve in terms of recruitment strategies. By embracing innovation and creativity, companies can differentiate themselves from competitors and attract the 'crème de la crème' job aspirants, who are drawn to forward-thinking organizations.

A study by the *Harvard Business Review* found that organizations using innovative interview techniques saw a

20% increase in employee performance post-hire.

4.
The Illusion of Simplicity: Deceptively Easy Questions

Not all questions are created equal. On the surface, some questions may appear deceptively simple, but beneath the façade interviewers are gauging your ability to think on your feet, navigate ambiguity, and approach problems with creativity.

What we discuss here will prepare you to confront the illusion of simplicity, where the line between simplicity and complexity becomes blurred. On one hand, deceptively easy questions may seem straightforward, inviting a straightforward response. They often lack the complexity and jargon associated with more technical or specialized queries. However, it's precisely this lack of complexity that belies the true nature of these questions. They're designed to probe deeper, to uncover the underlying thought processes, and to reveal the respondent's ability to think inventively.

On the other hand, surface-level responses to these

questions can be misleading, as they may initially appear satisfactory to the candidate. But, if you are able to critically analyze your answers post-interview, you may often find a lack of depth, a failure to consider alternative perspectives, and probably a lack of elaboration from your end. It's here that the contrast between surface-level and in-depth responses becomes stark.

"Ask any candidate how they think their interview went, and chances are that over 80% of them will sound very positive and confident in being able to answer all the questions. This optimism often plants the seed of disappointment when the outcome isn't what they expected."

To better understand this dichotomy, here are three examples of deceptively easy questions:
- *What's the most important quality you look for in a team member?*
- *How do you prioritize tasks when faced with multiple deadlines?*
- *If you could go back in time, what advice would you give to*

your younger self?

At first glance, these questions may seem innocuous, even simplistic. However, they're designed to elicit an answer that primarily reveals the respondent's thought processes. What they are not interested in is seeking a right or wrong answer. They require the respondent to think critically, to reflect on their experiences, and to articulate their thoughts in a clear and concise manner, demonstrating their clarity in communication.

The key strategy for the candidate is to recognize the importance of context. Easy questions often rely on context to provide depth and subtlety. By understanding the core context in which the question is being asked, respondents can tailor their answers to address the perspective from the 'other side of the table'.

Another strategy is to employ a structured approach when responding to these questions. This might involve breaking down the question into its component parts, identifying key variables, and developing a clear and concise narrative to walk the interviewer through the thought process. By doing so, respondents can demonstrate deeper understanding, and their ability to mold their stories to align with the desired perspective.

"By regularly practicing your skills and reflecting on your thought processes, you can develop a clearer, realistic understanding of your strengths and weaknesses, and identify areas where you may need to adapt or refine your mental approach. This approach enables you to think more critically and creatively, uncovering novel solutions and insights that might have otherwise remained hidden."

5.
The Creativity Quotient

What sparks the creative potential within us, and how can we leverage it to tackle the complex challenges of our time?

The answer lies at the intersection of cognitive psychology, neuroscience and innovative thinking, where the subtle interplay of curiosity, intrinsic motivation and diverse experiences converge, to ignite the creative spark. To better understand the catalysts of genius, we will briefly explore the psychological and cognitive triggers that foster innovative thinking.

Research suggests that curiosity, a natural human inclination, plays a pivotal role in sparking creativity. When we are curious, we're more likely to engage in exploratory behaviors, seeking out novel experiences and knowledge that can lead to innovative breakthroughs. Intrinsic motivation – the desire to solve a problem or create something meaningful – is another critical factor. When we're driven by a passion for discovery and a sense of purpose, we're more likely to persevere through challenges and push the boundaries of what's possible.

Diverse experiences are also essential for cultivating creative potential. When we're exposed to different cultures, perspectives and ways of thinking, our minds are able to form novel connections and generate innovative solutions. This is because our brains are wired to recognize patterns and relationships, and diverse experiences provide a rich array of stimuli, which can be woven together to create something new and original.

Consider the example of Steve Jobs, who drew inspiration from his experiences in calligraphy and design to create the revolutionary Macintosh computer. His early-life exposure to typography and design principles helped shape the innovative fonts and user-friendly design that became hallmarks of the Mac.

One of the most significant pitfalls of conventional thinking is the tendency to rely on established frameworks and mental models. When we're faced with a complex problem, it's tempting to reach for familiar solutions and tried methods, rather than taking the time to explore novel perspectives and possibilities. This can lead to a kind of intellectual stagnation, where we're unable to generate genuine innovative solutions.

Emotional intelligence: the human element in interviews.
Understanding the subtleties of emotions is necessary for effective communication, relationships and personal growth. We will briefly explore the critical terms and concepts that form the foundation of emotional intelligence.

The significance of grasping these terms cannot be overstated. By doing so, we can develop a deeper understanding of our own emotions, as well as those of others, enabling us to steer through complex social situations, build stronger relationships and make informed decisions.

Let us begin by examining the concept of emotional awareness, often referred to as the foundation of emotional intelligence. What exactly does it entail, and how can we cultivate it in our daily lives?

Emotional awareness refers to the ability to recognize, understand and acknowledge our emotions, as well as those of others. This involves developing a sensitivity to the subtleties of a situation, recognizing cues, and being conscious of how our emotions influence thoughts and behaviors. It is not just about being aware of emotions, but also understanding their underlying causes, identifying patterns and finding ways to manage them effectively.

'Emotional labeling' is the ability to clearly identify and label our emotions. Once individuals reach this level of awareness, they can process and understand their feelings more effectively, reducing the likelihood of emotional overwhelm. Acknowledgment and a better understanding of our emotions allow us to face challenging situations with a clearer mind and a more level-headed approach.

Another critical aspect of emotional awareness is empathy: the ability to understand and share the feelings of others. Empathy is not just about being sympathetic or feeling sorry for someone; rather, it involves actively engaging with another person's emotional experience, recognizing their perspectives and their needs, and acknowledging their emotions.

Let us briefly touch upon the concept of *'emotional regulation'*, which is the ability to manage and modulate our emotions in response to changing circumstances.

Emotional regulation is not about suppressing or denying our emotions, but rather about developing strategies to manage them effectively, ensuring that they do not dictate our thoughts and behaviors. By regulating our emotions, we can reduce stress, anxiety and emotional turmoil, leading to improved mental health and well-being.

One effective strategy for emotional regulation is mindfulness: the practice of being present in the moment, fully engaging with our experiences, and cultivating a non-judgmental awareness of our thoughts, feelings and bodily sensations. By practicing mindfulness, we can develop a greater sense of self-awareness, reduce emotional reactivity, and increase our ability to respond to challenging situations in a more thoughtful, intentional manner.

DRAWING CONCLUSIONS FROM CONTEXT.
Recognizing the pivotal role of context in shaping our understanding of interview questions.
The topics that we have covered so far would seem incomplete without mentioning the art of drawing meaningful conclusions from the context in which a question is asked, exploring the complexities of phrasing, tone and situational context.

Contextual clues: uncovering hidden meanings.

When faced with an interview question, it's easy to get caught up in the literal meaning of the words. However, it is the contextual clues that often reveal the underlying priorities and values sought by the interviewer. By recognizing and interpreting these clues, you can formulate answers that resonate on a deeper level, and align your mental wave-length with that of the interviewer.

A quick look at some of the contextual clues to watch out for:

Phrasing and tone:

Pay attention to the words and phrases used, as well as the tone and inflection of the interviewer's voice. For instance, a question phrased in a negative tone may indicate that the interviewer is seeking to understand your ability to handle challenges or criticisms.

An example question: *"What do you think is the biggest weakness of our company's current approach to customer service?"* Here, the negative tone and phrasing of the question suggest that the interviewer is seeking to understand your critical analysis skills and your ability to identify areas for improvement. By recognizing this contextual clue, you can compose your response to address the core concerns and demonstrate your comprehension.

Based on my personal experience, as a candidate and as an interviewer, carefully wording your responses and occasionally selecting the same or similar words taken from the question will create a profound, 'undefined' connection with the interviewer.

Situational context:

The situational context of an interview can also provide valuable clues about the interviewer's priorities and concerns. Consider the timing and setting of the interview, as well as any external factors that may be influencing the conversation.

As an example, if the company is undergoing a period of rapid growth or change, the interviewer may be seeking to focus on understanding your ability to adapt to new situations, and accept change receptively.

Consider the following example. You are being interviewed for a marketing position at a company that has recently undergone a major rebranding campaign. The interviewer asks: *"How do you stay up-to-date with the latest industry trends and developments?"* The situational context of the company's rebranding effort suggests that the interviewer is seeking to understand your ability to adapt to changing market conditions related to the rebranding, and how you prioritize your learning and development accordingly. By recognizing this contextual clue, you will be able to provide a thoughtful response that aligns with the interviewer's perspective, and highlights your adaptability and commitment to continuous learning.

Non-verbal cues – reading between the lines.
Observe the interviewer's body language, facial expressions and eye contact, which can signal their thoughts and feelings, allowing you to customize your answers dynamically, and engage more effectively in the conversation. However, you must never allow any of these elements displayed by the interviewer to distract you from maintaining a balanced composure and eye contact with the interviewer or panel.

Here are two example scenarios, to illustrate the critical aspects of behavioral indicators that highlight the significance of an interviewer's body language and visual signals.

First, the interviewer asks you about your experience in any particular relevant topic and, as you start your reply, you notice that they begin to nod and make eye contact. What does this non-verbal cue suggest?

Perhaps it indicates a growing interest in your response, or a desire to build rapport. Whatever the reason, by recognizing this cue, you can refine your response to foster an engaging and favorable interaction.

Second example: as you start responding to any question, you notice the interviewer glance at their watch and begin to shift in their seat. Such a non-verbal signal by the interviewer could indicate either one of these two likely interpretations:

- The interviewer is running low on time and wants to expedite the conversation.
- The interviewer is skeptical about your ability to provide a reasonably acceptable answer to this question, based on their assessment of your previous response to a similar question. This may be in case the question is more of a technical nature than a purely

behavioral question.

Previous questions – connecting the dots.
Take mental notes of the questions that have been asked previously during the session, as they may provide clues about the interviewer's priorities and concerns. By recognizing patterns or connections between questions, you can anticipate the interviewer's underlying focus and concerns, and adjust your responses accordingly. Here is an example that should help convey the point I'm aiming to illustrate.

The interviewer asks you about your experience with data analysis and, a few questions later, follows it up with a question about your ability to communicate complex ideas to non-technical stakeholders. What do these questions suggest about the interviewer's priorities? Most likely, they indicate a need for someone who can not only analyze data, but also communicate insights effectively when explaining them to a non-technical audience. By recognizing this pattern, you are already aware of the focus being on your 'communication' abilities and skills. Make sure to emphasize it, and you will be well-positioned to steer through the question with confidence and precision.

Tips and warnings.

When interpreting contextual clues, be cautious of making assumptions or jumping to conclusions. Contextual clues can be subtle and open to interpretation, so it's essential to consider the timing, context and consistency of the clues.

> *"Ultimately, as you prepare for your interview, it is imperative to cultivate a vigilant mindset, one that remains astutely attuned to the subtle clues and cues that may arise, for it is within these unspoken signals that your opportunity to connect and resonate with the interviewer lies."*

Silent signals – what are YOU saying without words?

Equally important is your awareness of the subtle contextual cues you may be projecting, and how they can be interpreted, significantly influencing the overall environment and shaping the interviewer's perception of you.

Ensure that your tone, body language and facial expressions are in harmony with your verbal statements, exuding confidence and enthusiasm. As I often emphasize to my clients and students, practicing your responses in front of a mirror remains one of the most effective methods for enhancing your delivery, improving your body language and identifying areas for refinement.

The power of pauses – using silence strategically.

Before moving on to the core subject of this book — the 55 questions and their answers — let's take a moment to explore a powerful yet often overlooked tool of communication: the strategic use of silence. This is a technique I frequently advise my students to harness during interviews.

Calculated silence—or, to be more precise, well-timed pauses—can be as telling as spoken words. Employing well-timed pauses in an interview creates moments of reflection, encourages interviewers to reveal more than they intended, and helps craft answers that hit the mark.

By incorporating purposeful pauses into your responses, you convey an impression of thoughtfulness and intentionality, signaling to the interviewer that your forthcoming words are closely grounded in reality. When you pause before answering, it conveys that you are weighing your thoughts, making your statements appear more factual and authentic. This not only enhances the credibility of your response but also engages the interviewer, prompting them to appreciate the depth of your insights.

One of my favorite questions to employ this technique is when asked to describe your strengths and weaknesses. Taking a moment to pause before responding to such a question signals to the interviewer that you are thoughtful and introspective, transforming what could be perceived as a rehearsed response into a genuine reflection. This brief interval not only enhances the authenticity of your answer, but also compels the interviewer to view your responses to other questions as being 'genuine' and closer to the truth.

THE 55 UNCONVENTIONAL QUESTIONS AND ANSWERS

Here is how the 55 questions and their answers are structured:

Q.: Behavioral and situational questions either related to specific professions, or broadly applicable to a variety of industries.

Motive: Three key skills that the interviewer seeks to assess.

Answer: Brief, targeted answers. Use of the storytelling method wherever possible, addressing the core-query, adding matter that resonates with the 'motive'.

Impact: The lasting impression aligned to the core skills that makes your answer impactful.

Maximizing your benefit from the questions and answers.
To derive the maximum benefit from the questions and answers, I encourage you to highlight the questions that resonate most with your profession or your industry, prioritizing them in your interview preparation.

Additionally, consider blending words and phrases from multiple answers, to create a more robust response that reflects your unique perspective.

Q1. *Tell us about a time you had to adapt your communication style to a specific audience.*

Motive: Communication adaptability. People awareness. Interpersonal skills.

Answer: *In one of my previous roles as an I.T. Data Analyst, I was tasked with presenting complex data analysis to a non-technical audience. Typically, I use jargon when communicating with colleagues, but in this case I recognized the need for simpler language and clear visuals for the presentation. I used analogies and focused on the impact of the data on our performance and business objectives. The audience was highly engaged and asked insightful questions, confirming that my approach was successful.*

Impact: Highlights adaptability, situational awareness, and tailoring communication for maximum impact.

Q2. *Describe a situation where you disagreed with a team decision. How did you voice your concerns and what was the outcome?*

Motive: Assertiveness. Diplomacy. Conflict resolution.

Answer: *During a regular brainstorming session at the start of a new project, the team was leaning toward a solution that lacked long-term scalability. The discussion was about an enlarged project team to start with. I politely interjected, presenting data and alternative approaches. I emphasized the importance of future-proofing our decision through past data. The team appreciated the additional perspective, and we ultimately adopted a hybrid solution that addressed both immediate needs and the roadmap for the project.*

Impact: Demonstrates the ability to collaborate effectively while advocating for a well-reasoned alternative. A strong leadership trait.

Q3. *You witness a colleague taking credit for someone else's work. How do you handle this situation?*

Motive: Integrity. Ethics. Issue resolution.

Answer: *I would first discreetly approach the erring colleague and have a one-to-one, privately explaining what I had witnessed. This would allow the colleague the freedom to express their perspective. Depending on their reaction, I would either encourage them to address it directly with the manager or, if they remain hesitant, I would inform the manager myself, ensuring proper credit is given where it is due. As a manager, I would follow the same initial steps of privately discussing it with the concerned staff member. Once we reach an agreement, I would make sure to openly recognize their contribution within the team, ensuring that their efforts are acknowledged by all.*

Impact: Shows commitment to ethical conduct, prioritizing a solution that encourages honesty in the workplace.

Q4. *Imagine you're tasked with a project requiring a specific skill set that you lack. How do you approach this challenge?*

Motive: Quick learning. Initiative. Can-do attitude.

Answer: *My first step would be to research how I can acquire the required skills through whatever resources may be available, including online research and industry publications. I would also utilize the expertise of colleagues from the concerned work area or department within our organization, seeking their advice or requesting shadowing opportunities. Additionally, I would proactively look out for any in-house training modules or short courses, to help me improve my skillset and demonstrate my commitment to grow through learning.*

Impact: Highlights strong initiative, self-directed learning, resourcefulness and commitment to growth.

Q5. *Our company values a culture of continuous improvement. How can you contribute to this in your role?*

Motive: Initiative. Problem identification. Adaptability.

Answer: *I'm a strong believer in ongoing improvements, through analyzing various contributing factors and implementing a multi-pronged approach. I would actively seek opportunities to streamline work processes and practices, identifying areas for potential gains in output, productivity and quality, through automation or implementing change where required. Conducting regular team brainstorming sessions and anonymous online surveys, to gather broader feedback, and encouraging inputs and suggestions, are very strong methods of introducing new ideas collaboratively, which also fosters an environment of motivation through participation. It is also important to have a robust management commitment toward change implementation, when and where required.*

Impact: Demonstrates a proactive mindset and commitment to continuous growth, through collaboration and teamwork.

Q6. *What motivates you to excel in your career?*

Motive: Goal orientation. Drive and ambition. Clarity of vision.

Answer: *Beyond the daily routine tasks, I'm intrinsically motivated by observing my work contributing toward a larger objective. I feel energized by opportunities to learn new skills, tackle complex challenges and contribute to innovative solutions that have a lasting impact on the organization's success. But, the most impactful motivation throughout my career has been the opportunity to take on additional responsibilities, as it reflects the company's trust and confidence in my abilities.*

Impact: Focus on long-term goals. Continuous learning. Leadership.

Q7. *Describe a time you had to prioritize competing deadlines. How did you manage your time effectively?*

Motive: Prioritization. Time management. Collaboration.

Answer: *In one of my previous roles as a Site Supervisor, I once faced overlapping deadlines on two critical projects. My first action was to amend the schedules for both projects, highlighting the key milestones and allocating realistic timeframes for each of them. Next, I communicated the challenges clearly with the team allocated under my supervision, and with all concerned stakeholders, setting realistic expectations and requesting flexibility where required. Moreover, I also leveraged collaboration, delegating additional tasks to team members who possessed multiple skill sets. This method, and the teamwork we achieved, ensured that both projects were completed without any delay and to a high standard.*

Impact: Strong time-management, communication and collaboration skills.

Q8. *How do you stay up to date on industry trends and advancements relevant to your field?*

Motive: Professional development. Continuous learning. Growth mindset.

Answer: *I prioritize continuous learning at all times, regularly searching and attending webinars or professional talk events that I can attend, based on my available time and schedule. Subscribing to industry-related publications is a top priority for me, as I am an avid reader during my spare time. I have a notable presence on a number of professional online forums and communities, where I connect with industry experts. Utilizing company resources, like training modules or programs, is another way that I seek opportunities to stay ahead of the curve.*

Impact: Demonstrates a commitment to continuous improvement through learning and staying relevant.

Q9. *Imagine you receive conflicting instructions from two different managers about the same task. How would you navigate this situation?*

Motive: Problem-solving. Diplomacy. Overcoming complex situations.

Answer: *First, I would clarify the objectives and deadline of the task or the project. I would then seek to meet with both managers to understand the rationale behind their instructions, and to identify any potential overlap or conflicting priorities. This situation could arise due to a lack of communication between both managers, therefore I would try to facilitate the communication between them, aiming for a solution that aligns closely with the project objectives and better business interest. It would be imperative for me to keep both managers informed about my action plan and priorities, and to keep them periodically updated about the project's progress.*

Impact: Task-focused. Communication mastery and strong problem-resolution skills, in a potentially complex situation.

Q10. *If you were authorized to create a new role in the company, what would it be and why?*

Motive: Innovation. Leadership. Foresight.

Answer: *I would begin by analyzing the company's current goals, and any emerging challenges or opportunities in the industry. With that in mind, I would propose a role focused on enhancing cross-functional collaboration — perhaps a 'floating' role of 'Strategic Innovation Lead', who could bridge gaps between departments, such as product development, R&D, marketing and technology. This role would ensure that new ideas and initiatives align with current and forecasted market demands and company strategy, driving innovation and creating competitive advantages. By fostering communication and encouraging innovation, this role would help unlock untapped potential and contribute to the company's long-term business growth.*

Impact: A forward-thinking mindset, deep understanding of company growth drivers, and the ability to conceptualize new strategies that align with business goals.

Q11. *Describe a situation where you had to explain a complex concept to someone with limited knowledge in that area. How did you ensure they understood the idea?*

Motive: Communication clarity. Adaptability. Empathy.

Answer: *In a previous role as a product marketing manager, I had to explain the operating features of one of our machinery to a sales team from another company, whose main business was not related to this product, but they had bulk-purchased this item from us. To ensure that they fully understood, I broke down the product's key features into everyday terms, using comparisons to familiar everyday use tools. It sounded innovative and sometimes humorous to them, but my objective was achieved. I also provided step-by-step demonstrations, allowing them to follow along. Throughout the session, I checked in frequently, encouraging them to ask questions. This approach ensured that, by the end of my presentation, they had a solid understanding of the product features, and felt confident in promoting it effectively.*

Impact: Displays communication adaptability, audience awareness, agility and innovation.

Q12. *How would you handle a situation where you believe a colleague is underperforming?*

Motive: Leadership. Interpersonal communication. Emotional intelligence.

Answer: *I would first approach the colleague privately, express my observations and offer my support, without sounding negative. It is best to allow the colleague to identify the underlying reasons for their weaker areas, which can usually be addressed through specific training, mentoring or shadowing a senior, to gain confidence and uplift the output and productivity. If necessary, I would escalate the matter to the H.R. L&D, to provide support to the staff through a structured performance improvement program.*

Impact: High level of collaboration, leadership and interpersonal skills.

NOTE:

If you have so far found these questions and their answers valuable, I would be grateful if you could take a moment to leave a review on the platform where you purchased this book. Your thoughts not only support my journey as an author but also help fellow readers make informed choices. Thank you.

Q13. *How do you deal with being highly appreciated and awarded?*

Motive: Humility. Work ethic. Appreciation.

Answer: *I view each recognition as a stepping-stone, not a destination. Receiving recognition for my work is always humbling and motivating. It acknowledges my effort and reinforces the value I bring to the team. I always attribute even the minor successes to the colleagues or seniors who either supported me directly or provided guidance for me to attain any achievements. I express my sincere gratitude to those who offered the appreciation or awarded me. It fuels my commitment to continuous improvement, and motivates me to strive for higher goals in future.*

Impact: Demonstrates humility, teamwork and a strong work ethic.

Q14. *How do you approach giving constructive feedback to a colleague?*

Motive: Interpersonal communication. Leadership. Emotional intelligence.

Answer: *When providing feedback, I prioritize a positive and supportive style. I focus on specific behaviors or actions, and suggest alternative approaches toward achieving progress. Before bringing up the areas for improvement, I would offer appreciation and highlight the colleague's strengths. This approach ensures that the feedback is received openly, sounds constructive and fosters growth for the colleague. It is also a good time to invite suggestions from the colleague, in case they would be open to receiving specific support, in the form of specified training or mentoring. This discussion would always take place in a private environment.*

Impact: Demonstrates strong emotional intelligence and effective communication, and focuses on growth and development.

Q15. *Describe a time when you had to overcome a significant obstacle in achieving a goal. What did you learn from the experience?*

Motive: Resilience. Adaptability. Self-reflection.

Answer: *During a project, in one of my last roles as an I.T. Training Manager, we encountered an unexpected technical glitch that threatened our course deadline. I researched solutions, collaborated with colleagues from the sections that were impacted, and explored alternative approaches. We ultimately overcame the obstacle by adapting our strategy and rescheduling some low-priority project milestones. This experience taught me the importance of resourcefulness, resilience, and the power of teamwork in overcoming challenges.*

Impact: High level of resourcefulness, problem-solving and collaboration.

Q16. *How do you stay motivated and focused during long or challenging projects?*

Motive: Work ethic. Self-management. Perseverance.

Answer: *I maintain motivation by setting gradual milestones and celebrating achievements along the way. I also break down large tasks into smaller, manageable steps. When facing challenges, I remind myself of the project's overall goal and its significance for our business. Regular sharing of progressive, key milestones with project team members serves as a powerful motivator, fostering a sense of collective accomplishment and sustained enthusiasm. This practice not only reinforces team cohesion but also helps maintain high morale, and a focused drive toward our ultimate project objectives.*

Impact: Displays a goal-oriented mindset, teamwork and self-motivation.

Q17. *Imagine receiving negative feedback on your work. How would you react and what would you do next?*

Motive: Resilience. Adaptability. Confidence.

Answer: *I have an open outlook, and appreciate constructive criticism as an opportunity for growth. I have developed a three-step method to tackle such a situation. First, I would actively listen to the feedback. Second, I would clarify any unclear points and, if required, present my perspective. And, finally, I would self-analyze the feedback to identify areas for improvement, and where I could learn to do better. It is all about continuous improvement. Additionally, if the feedback is provided by someone with more than my experience, I would seek guidance to ensure I fully understand the expectations, and implement the necessary changes.*

Impact: Demonstrates a growth mindset, openness to feedback and continuous learning.

Q18. *How do you manage a healthy work-life balance for yourself?*

Motive: Self-awareness. Time management. Professional commitment.

Answer: *For me, a healthy work-life balance means prioritizing efficiency and focus during work hours. Over a period of time, I have gained an expertise in prioritizing my work effectively, which is the result of conscious efforts and practice. Outside of work, I maintain a healthy schedule that includes quality family time, activities for relaxation and personal development. This balance allows me to return to work feeling refreshed, and keeps me motivated every Monday.*

Impact: Highlights time-management skills, self-awareness and the importance of personal well-being.

Q19. *Describe a time you had to learn a new skill quickly. How did you approach the learning process?*

Motive: Adaptability. Agility. Quick learning.

Answer: *When a new software program became essential to my role, I actively sought out learning resources before it was actually implemented in my department. This was during one of my previous jobs at a software development firm. I researched and completed online tutorials at home, utilized company training materials, and even reached out to colleagues with expertise in the upcoming program. I practiced the new skill diligently, and asked questions to ensure I fully understood its functionalities and what it had to offer. This approach allowed me to become proficient in the new software quickly and efficiently. I was also fortunate that the company had a proactive approach toward training, arranging briefing sessions for teams from various departments, prior to the launch.*

Impact: Self-initiative, resourcefulness and a strong learning mindset.

Q20. *How do you handle a situation where you disagree with a company policy?*

Motive: Professional ethics. Critical thinking. Adaptability.

Answer: *If I disagree with a policy, I would first research its rationale and the underlying purpose of its implementation. If I believe my concerns hold validity, I would address them to H.R. through appropriate channels. Instead of only expressing my disagreement with it, I would make sure to offer constructive solutions or suggest alternative approaches to achieve the policy objectives. I would offer to collaborate with management to explore potential revisions to the policy in future, showcasing professionalism and a willingness to find solutions.*

Impact: High level of professionalism, critical thinking and effective communication.

Q21. *Imagine you're tasked with leading a team with diverse backgrounds and working styles. How would you ensure a collaborative environment?*

Motive: Leadership. Inclusivity. Communication.

Answer: *I would foster collaboration by establishing clear goals and expectations for the team, right from the start. I would make sure to encourage open communication and invite ideas, creating a safe space for everyone to share their perspectives. One key tactic I use within teams is never to outright dismiss or negate ideas from team members, even if they may not seem relevant or acceptable for implementation. I would provide my honest feedback, with justifiable reasoning about why the idea cannot be accepted. Another important factor is to leverage the team's diverse strengths, by assigning tasks that capitalize on individual skillsets. Additionally, I would celebrate successes that highlight the team's collective effort, which ensures keeping all members equally motivated and focused.*

Impact: Diversity and inclusivity awareness. Leadership. Interpersonal communication.

Q22. *Our company prioritizes innovation. Describe a time you came up with a creative solution to a problem.*

Motive: Initiative. Problem solving. Strategic thinking.

Answer: *In one of my previous roles as a Warehouse Supervisor, we faced a recurring logistical challenge. I analyzed the problem from different angles and brainstormed solutions with colleagues. Forming a core action team of three colleagues, we distributed daily tasks to monitor and record the issue for evaluation. Based on a five-day analysis of the issue, I proposed an amendment to one of the processes, which leveraged underutilized resources and streamlined the flow of work. This solution not only resolved the issue but also improved efficiency and the output, in terms of manpower and equipment utilization.*

Impact: Demonstrates problem-solving skills, creativity and a collaborative approach to innovation.

Q23. *How do you measure your own success in the workplace?*

Motive: Self-awareness. Goal setting. Accountability.

Answer: *Measuring my own success is based on a combination of factors. Beyond meeting deadlines, I assess my progress by the impact of my work on the overall project objectives. I also make sure to track my own growth, in terms of acquiring new skills and mastering existing ones. Moreover, I value and encourage regular feedback from colleagues and clients, which I use as a measurement tool of my performance, effectiveness, and my contributions toward the organizational goals.*

Impact: Positive mindset. Highlights a focus on continuous learning and accountability.

Q24. *Describe a time you had to delegate tasks to colleagues. How did you ensure they had the necessary skills and support?*

Motive: Delegation. Teamwork. Communication.

Answer: *When delegating tasks, I start by ensuring clear communication about the expectations, timelines and the desired outcome. I assign work after assessing each team member's strengths, based on their past performance, experience level and specific training qualification in various areas of work. Making sure to provide them with the necessary resources and support is extremely critical. I maintain open communication channels, to address any questions or concerns as they arise.*

Impact: Demonstrates effective delegation skills, task focus and fostering team success.

Q25. *How do you stay organized and manage multiple tasks simultaneously?*

Motive: Time management. Organization. Work discipline.

Answer: *I prioritize tasks based on urgency and importance. To be honest, I have pasted a printed copy of the 'Eisenhower Matrix' next to my workstation, which clearly categorizes tasks into four categories: 'Urgent and Important', 'Not Urgent but Important', 'Urgent but Not Important', and 'Not Urgent and Not Important'; a quick glance at this table guides me, in only a few seconds, on which work to focus on, and keeps me on track. I also schedule dedicated time slots for routine daily work, to avoid any pile-up or delays. These steps allow me to manage multiple projects efficiently and meet deadlines consistently.*

Impact: Effective organization, time-management and prioritization skills.

Q26. *Can you walk us through your background, and experiences that make you a strong candidate for this role?*

Motive: Self-awareness. Confidence. Role suitability.

Answer: *Absolutely! My professional journey has been shaped by* (it is best to mention relevant past experiences aligned to the new job role). *These experiences have allowed me to develop strong skills in* (mention key skills relevant to this role). *Having conducted research on many companies during my job search, I am particularly drawn to this opportunity at your company, because the role resonates with my experience and my future career goals. I believe my skills, enthusiasm and concept of teamwork would be a valuable asset to your organization, and I'm eager to not only contribute toward achieving the responsibilities assigned to this role, but to excel as a role model for my co-workers.*

Impact: Strong confidence level. Self-motivation. Displays initiative and good communication skills.

Q27. *Our company values data-driven decision-making. How do you approach analyzing data to keep your work updated?*

Motive: Analytical thinking. Technical proficiency. Decision-making based on evidence

Answer: *I leverage data analysis to gain insights for making informed decisions. I am comfortable working with various data sets and utilizing relevant tools to analyze trends, and to identify patterns and vulnerabilities. I focus on drawing meaningful conclusions from the data, and use these insights to develop effective solutions. Keeping myself updated with the new releases or enhancements is also very important for me, which I achieve through the available in-house resources.*

Impact: Demonstrates analytical thinking, comfort with data analysis, and using data to drive decision-making.

Q28. *How do you handle a situation where a colleague takes credit for your work?*

Motive: Professionalism. Assertiveness. Conflict resolution.

Answer: *If a colleague takes credit for my work, I would approach them privately and calmly explain the situation. It would be important for me to have the documentation or other relevant evidence readily available to support my point. My goal would be to ensure that proper credit is acknowledged where it is due, focusing on a solution for moving forward, rather than creating conflict. I would escalate the issue if not resolved through my direct contact with the co-worker.*

Impact: High level of professional maturity, assertive behavior and prioritizing a positive outcome.

Q29. *Imagine facing a situation where you have limited resources to complete a project. How would you approach this challenge?*

Motive: Resourcefulness. Problem solving. Adaptability.

Answer: *This is a common issue faced by many experienced professionals. With limited resources, I would be compelled to prioritize tasks strictly, and identify the areas where I could optimize efficiency. I would also explore creative solutions, such as leveraging free online tools or collaborating with colleagues to share resources. Efficient delegation of responsibilities to the right team members greatly helps in such situations. Additionally, I would be proactive in seeking alternative resources from within the company, demonstrating resourcefulness while ensuring timely completion of the project.*

Impact: Prioritization. Organizational skills. Resolution-based mindset.

Q30. *How do you define ethical conduct in the workplace?*

Motive: Professionalism. Work ethics. Integrity.

Answer: *To me, ethical conduct in the work environment basically means honesty, integrity and fairness in all of our interactions. It involves upholding company policies on codes of conduct and avoiding conflict of interest, when performing our duties and carrying out our assigned responsibilities. It also means respecting colleagues and clients, treating everyone with dignity. Ultimately, ethical conduct fosters trust and ensures a positive, productive and healthy work environment.*

Impact: Strong understanding of ethical principles and dignity. Upholding organizational reputation.

Q31. *Describe a time when you had to go above and beyond your job description to achieve a positive outcome. What motivated you to take that extra step?*

Motive: Initiative. Dedication. Drive to excel.

Answer: *In my first job as an Airport Operations Junior, I noticed a recurring issue within a specific process, which was causing problems for passengers travelling with excessive baggage, and also caused flight delays in some cases. While it wasn't directly part of my job responsibility, I felt compelled to find a solution. Since I had just started my career and I was eager to learn, I stayed back after my working hours and researched solutions and best practices, often going through the complete process myself, as a passenger. Surprisingly, there were quite a few yet-unidentified potential process improvements I could highlight when looking at it from the customers' perspective. I presented my findings and the proposed changes to my manager, which were all accepted. This initiative not only addressed the issue, but also resulted in significant time savings for us and the travelers. I still hold the certificate of appreciation I received, with pride and a sense of achievement.*

Impact: Innovative approach. Displays self-motivation and empathy.

Q32. *How do you approach giving and receiving feedback?*

Motive: Diplomacy. Adaptability. Receptiveness.

Answer: *I consider feedback as the 'mirror of personal growth'. While providing feedback, it is preferable to create a constructive and supportive environment. The emphasis must remain on specific behaviors and actions, offering suggestions for improvement while acknowledging the colleague's strengths. I also frame feedback as a learning opportunity, encouraging open communication and questions. One of the basics that I follow is to first highlight the positives then discuss the areas of improvement. When receiving feedback, active listening, acknowledging and expressing my appreciation for the insights are the most important actions to take. I reflect on the feedback, and identify areas for personal and professional growth, demonstrating my commitment to continuous learning.*

Impact: Empathetic approach. Leadership. Receptiveness.

Q33. *Tell us about a time when you needed to compromise on quality at work, and why. How did you manage the situation?*

Motive: Adaptability. Prioritization. Communication clarity.

Answer: *In a previous role, I was tasked with completing a complex project with two major challenges: a tight deadline and the absence of some key team members, who were either on vacation or assigned to other, larger projects. While maintaining the highest-quality standards and the delivery schedule is always my priority, in this instance I had to make some minor adjustments to the project milestones delivery, which I communicated directly to the stakeholders, right at the project's start, explaining the rationale behind it. We also needed to reschedule some tasks that could be completed post-project delivery. Being proactive and adaptable, we managed to complete the core project within the schedule, and my transparency in communication was actually appreciated by all parties involved.*

Impact: Adaptability, prioritizing deadlines, and effectively communicating under challenging situations.

Q34. *If you were asked to present a complex technical idea to a non-technical audience, how would you ensure clear communication?*

Motive: Situational awareness. Communication adaptability. Empathy.

Answer: *I would tailor my presentation to the audience's level of understanding, using clear, concise language, and avoid technical jargon, leveraging relatable analogies and visuals to enhance comprehension. In the case of a presentation, color-coding different terms and the use of non-technical graphic visuals often make it easier to grasp. Additionally, I would encourage questions throughout the session, to ensure that everyone is on board. By creating an open and interactive environment, I can gauge the audience's understanding and adjust my approach accordingly, ensuring that the complex idea is communicated effectively and resonates with the entire group.*

Impact: Adaptability. Clear communication and audience engagement skills.

Q35. *What is your understanding of 'service recovery' when dealing with customers?*

Motive: Problem resolution. Customer handling. Listening.

Answer: *Service recovery is about turning a negative customer experience into a positive one. It's not just about fixing the immediate problem, but also about restoring the customer's trust and confidence in the product, service and brand. Effective service recovery involves acknowledging the issue and being a good listener, taking swift and appropriate action to resolve it, and offering alternative options, in case the promised delivery cannot be fulfilled. This makes the client feel valued and heard. It's an opportunity to demonstrate our commitment to customer satisfaction, and it often turns them into loyal clients.*

Impact: Empathy. Customer-centric approach. Ability to turn challenges into opportunities.

Q36. *How do you define a positive company culture, and how would you contribute to it?*

Motive: Comprehension. Flexibility. Team spirit.

Answer: *For me, a positive company culture fosters collaboration, respect and open communication channels. It's a culture that values continuous learning, providing employees with easily accessible resources for growth and development. One of the most critical elements of such an environment is that every team member feels empowered. I would contribute to this environment by being a trusted team player, supportive colleague, a source of positivity and a troubleshooter, whenever required. Offering support and mentorship to junior team members is a priority for me. I would also actively participate in company initiatives and promote open communication, spreading a sense of belonging and shared purpose.*

Impact: Clarity of definitions and goals. Team player and a leader.

Q37. *If you receive an unexpected task, with no clear instructions, how would you approach this situation?*

Motive: Solutions-based mindset. Initiative. Resourcefulness.

Answer: If I receive an unexpected task, with no clear instructions, I wouldn't hesitate to grab the opportunity of accepting it. First, I would clarify the overall goal, its desired outcome, and the resources allocated to complete the project, by reaching out to the person who assigned the task to me. After gathering all the relevant information, I would then research the necessary information about the required framework of skills and resources for the task. If necessary, I would seek guidance from colleagues with expertise in that area. This proactive approach would ensure that I understand the task fully, and am well-equipped to complete it successfully.

Impact: Can-do attitude. Continuous learning ability, adaptability and resourcefulness.

Q38. *Imagine a situation where a colleague isn't pulling their weight on a team project, or not contributing enough. How would you address this situation?*

Motive: Teamwork. Conflict resolution. Fostering accountability.

Answer: For any colleague who is not contributing enough to meet expectations on a project, my initial action would be direct communication with them privately. This would be a high priority for me to take immediate action. I would express my concerns in a respectful and constructive manner, presenting facts and figures if applicable, focusing on the specific issues and the potential impact on the project's overall success. I would also encourage the team member to openly communicate their perspectives and any underlying causes of the issue. Based on the employee's response and our overall discussion, I would offer support and explore ways to help them improve their performance through training, shadowing, or any other means specific to the situation. The next important step for me would be to monitor the situation closely and, in case the situation persists, involve the team lead or manager, to discuss potential solutions and ensure project accountability for everyone involved.

Impact: Issue resolution, empathy and transparent

communication. High level of fairness and accountability.

Q39. *Describe a time you had to deal with a difficult client or customer. How did you manage the situation and achieve a positive outcome?*

Motive: Customer handling. Problem solving. Emotional intelligence.

Answer: *In a previous role, where I was assigned to the items return center, I encountered an upset couple who felt their concerns were being ignored. I immediately sensed their main concern and stopped all my work to give them my full attention, listening to them attentively until they finished their conversation. By acknowledging their frustration and actively engaging, I could sense their demeanor shift as they felt heard. This is a technique that I often use in such situations. I then identified the root cause and explored some creative solutions, offering multiple options to provide them with a sense of choice and control. Offering options helps in such cases, where you may be unable to provide an immediate solution to their issue. Through clear communication and a positive approach, I was able to de-escalate the situation, and successfully turned their negative perception into a positive impression, restoring their confidence in our customer service.*

Impact: Conflict resolution. Communication (listening),

diplomacy and a high level of empathy.

Q40. *How do you approach setting goals for yourself, both professionally and personally?*

Motive: Goal setting. Vision. Work-life balance.

Answer: *I believe in setting both short- and long-term goals to maintain focus, motivation and self-discipline. Since many years ago, when I started utilizing the SMART goal framework – ensuring my goals are Specific, Measurable, Achievable, Relevant and Time-bound – this method helps me to get back on track, if I ever feel either off-track or demotivated. I regularly review and revise the path I tread toward my goals, ensuring that they align with my professional and personal aspirations. This approach allows me to achieve progress in both areas, and maintain a healthy work-life balance.*

Impact: Clarity of vision. Professionalism. Self-care.

Q41. *How do you define your success in a work project?*

Motive: Goal setting. Accountability. Attention to detail.

Answer: *For me, success goes beyond just meeting deadlines. It's about achieving the project's ultimate objectives while promoting a positive work environment. A successful project delivers value to all stakeholders, meets expectations and contributes to business growth. My focus during a project is also to encourage collaboration and learning within the participants, enhancing team spirit, motivation and cohesion.*

Impact: Leadership. Focus on results, collaboration and teamwork. Showcasing a broader understanding of success.

Q42. *Reflect on a situation when you took the lead on a project without being formally assigned. What motivated you and what was the result?*

Motive: Initiative. Leadership. Self-motivation.

Answer: *In one of my previous roles as an Events Planning Manager, a high-profile, ongoing project was falling behind schedule, due to a lack of clarity about the project ownership. Before long, I recognized the impact this would have on our client's satisfaction, the team's workload and the qualitative project outcome. Since I was newly recruited and I wanted to highlight my leadership skills, I voluntarily stepped in to coordinate the efforts between certain suppliers and the technical staff, where the issues had cropped up. By organizing regular check-ins, redistributing tasks based on the team members' experience and strengths, and maintaining a positive environment, we not only met the deadline but also exceeded the client's expectations. My motivation stemmed from a desire to ensure the team's success, and to attain the recognition of my strengths as a new employee.*

Impact: Highlights initiative and leadership, demonstrating a proactive approach and a commitment to organizational success.

Q43. *How do you define success while working in a team environment?*

Motive: Teamwork. Collaboration. Diversity.

Answer: *Success in a team environment goes well beyond individual achievements and performance. It's about achieving a shared goal through effective collaboration, communication and mutual support. A successful team leverages its collective strengths, celebrates milestones together, and learns from both successes and challenges. Ultimately, it's about achieving the desired outcome while promoting a positive and productive work environment. In addition, working with a team of individuals from diverse backgrounds brings a broader range of ideas, perspectives and skills to the table, driving innovation and a more creative approach to problem-solving. This inclusiveness not only enriches the decision-making process, but also encourages a work culture that respects and values different viewpoints. Ultimately, it's about achieving the desired outcome while promoting a positive and productive work environment.*

Impact: Strong collaboration and communication abilities. Highlights the value of teamwork, diversity and inclusion.

Q44. *Can you describe a time when you had to adapt to a significant change at work? What steps did you take to manage the transition smoothly?*

Motive: Adaptability. Resilience. Change management.

Answer: *Changes always come with challenges. At my previous job, we underwent a sudden organizational restructure, which required some of my team members to take on new responsibilities with minimal notice, due to workforce downsizing. Being the head of my section, I was notified about it a few days in advance of the announcement. My first thought was to schedule a series of quick training and briefing sessions, in coordination with the Learning and Development colleagues, to ensure that everyone reached the required skill levels within a minimum period. This meant that the targeted-training-sessions schedule was announced at the same time the restructuring details were broadcast to all staff. During the daily morning pep-talk, I encouraged open communication, to address any staff concerns and to offer immediate support. I recall having to stay back with some co-workers well over the normal working hours, for over two weeks, only to ensure that all concerns and lack of confidence in the team were addressed. Through proactively managing expectations and creating a support system, we not only adapted to the change but also improved our overall* *efficiency, productivity and employee morale.*

Impact: High level of adaptability, leadership and change-management skills.

Q45. *If you receive a more lucrative offer from another company, shortly after starting with us, how would you approach this situation?*

Motive: Decision-making. Loyalty. Integrity.

Answer: *In such a scenario, my first reaction would be to evaluate the new offer against my current role, in terms of growth potential, the cultural fit, and alignment with my future career plans. I value the commitment that I would have already made with you, and I would seek an open conversation with my immediate superior about the situation, expressing my enthusiasm for the ongoing projects undertaken by me. If the conversation leads to an understanding of mutual growth, without any binding commitments on either side, I would prioritize staying committed to my current role, aware of the fact that job satisfaction and alignment with my long-term goals outweigh immediate financial gains.*

Impact: Thoughtful decision-making. Highlights integrity, honesty and organizational commitment.

Q46. *How do you handle a situation where you're assigned a task that you don't feel completely qualified for?*

Motive: Learning agility. Self-awareness. Growth mindset.

Answer: *I view challenges as opportunities for growth. When assigned a task outside my expertise, I begin by assessing my current knowledge and skills, to determine the best course of action. My next step would be to actively seek company-provided training resources, consult with colleagues who have the relevant expertise, and explore online learning methods. I believe these actions will boost my confidence and enable me to start on the right footing, while continuing to learn as the project progresses. After completing the task, I would ensure to acknowledge the team members who supported me, and appreciate the opportunity to expand my skills and professional experience.*

Impact: A can-do attitude. Continuous learning and a sense of appreciation.

Q47. *Describe a time you leveraged technology to improve a process or solve a problem.*

Motive: Innovation. Technical proficiency. Collaboration.

Answer: *In a previous role as a Software Marketing Manager, we encountered inefficiencies in data analysis, due to manual processes in certain areas which negatively impacted our manpower utilization and team productivity. Collaborating with the I.T. team responsible for the software, I researched automation tools, and together we identified a support program that could streamline and automate a significant portion of the processes. The software add-on incurred additional costs, so I partnered with our finance team to conduct a cost-to-productivity analysis, justifying the investment. I led the initiative to adopt the new system, trained colleagues on its functionalities, and successfully implemented it across all branches. This resulted in faster data analysis, enhanced accuracy and optimized resource utilization.*

Impact: Data-driven decision-making. Business acumen. Resourcefulness.

Q48. *How do you handle a situation where you've made a mistake at work?*

Motive: Accountability. Continuous learning. Self-analysis.

Answer: *Everyone makes mistakes, and the key is acknowledgement and knowing how to learn from them. If I make a mistake, I take full accountability and prioritize rectifying the situation as quickly and effectively as possible. I would communicate the issue transparently to those impacted, and turn my focus toward working on the solution. Later, I would analyze the cause of the error and address the shortfall, to prevent similar mistakes in the future, demonstrating my commitment to continuous improvement and learning.*

Impact: Displays self-analysis and ownership. Continuous learning mindset.

Q49. *Describe your experience working in a fast-paced environment. How do you stay focused and manage stress under pressure?*

Motive: Adaptability. Resilience. Stress management.

Answer: *Actually, I thrive in fast-paced environments and enjoy the challenge of handling multiple tasks simultaneously. I am skilled at prioritizing effectively, and utilize time-management tools to stay organized. The real challenge occurs when unexpected issues or situations pop up, which can potentially disrupt my work schedule. That is where maintaining clear and transparent communication with colleagues and stakeholders is extremely critical. To manage stress, I make sure to prioritize breaks throughout the day, to maintain a healthy balance between work and relaxation. Discussing ongoing projects and critical tasks with team members, during our breaks, can also serve as a great stress-reliever. This allows me to stay focused, maintain a positive attitude and deliver high-quality work, even under pressure.*

Impact: Resilience. Clear prioritization and stress-management techniques.

Q50. *Our company is committed to diversity and inclusion. How would you contribute to a positive and inclusive work environment?*

Motive: Teamwork. Empathy. Cultural sensitivity.

Answer: *I believe diversity and inclusion are essential for a thriving workplace. I would contribute by encouraging an environment of respect and appreciation for different backgrounds, perspectives and cultures. In my current role, I have already formed two small groups of colleagues assigned to work on resolving minor issues as troubleshooters, and I made it a point to combine employees from varied backgrounds. I actively listen to them, embrace open communication, and celebrate the unique strengths that each individual brings to the team. Additionally, this provides me with the opportunity to learn about different perspectives and mindsets, promoting a truly inclusive environment, where everyone feels valued and empowered to contribute.*

Impact: Inclusiveness and diversity awareness. Teamwork and empathy.

Q51. *What motivates you to come to work every day?*

Motive: Passion. Self-motivation. Clarity of purpose.

Answer: *Beyond the daily tasks, I'm intrinsically motivated by a sense of purpose, and the opportunity to contribute to something bigger than myself. I find it rewarding to contribute toward solving problems, to continuously learn and grow, and making a positive impact whenever the opportunity arises. Mentoring less experienced team members provides me with an added boost of energy. Dividing my tasks into smaller milestones sustains my motivation, ensuring I eagerly anticipate each new day. I also enjoy the collaborative environment and the camaraderie of working alongside talented colleagues, all working toward shared goals.*

Impact: Professional commitment. Displays extraordinary sense of purpose, teamwork and motivation.

Q52. *Describe a time you had to deal with a situation where ethical considerations clashed with company expectations. How did you navigate this challenge?*

Motive: Integrity. Decision-making. Navigating complex situations.

Answer: *This is a sensitive issue, and so far in my career I have not come across such a situation directly. If faced with a situation where ethics clash with company policy or expectations, I would prioritize upholding my ethical principles. To begin with, I would gather all the facts and thoroughly understand the situation from both perspectives. Secondly, I would attempt to communicate my concerns to my manager or to the H.R. business partner, proposing alternative solutions that align with both company goals and ethical considerations. If necessary, I would be prepared to explain my reasoning and potentially seek external guidance, to ensure a fair and ethical outcome.*

Impact: Leadership. High moral values and diplomacy.

Q53. *How do you define effective leadership, and how would you demonstrate these qualities in this role?*

Motive: Leadership style. Leadership principles. Assertiveness.

Answer: *Effective leadership, to me, is about inspiring and motivating others to align with a vision, and directing combined efforts toward shared goals. Key elements of good leadership include clear communication, encouraging collaboration, strategic delegation, and empowering team members to maximize their strengths. It also involves offering timely feedback, guidance and support, to help individuals thrive. In this role, I would exemplify these qualities by actively listening to team members, cultivating a supportive environment through shared responsibilities, and delegating tasks with intention. Additionally, I would celebrate achievements, and promote continuous learning and development, to nurture the team's long-term growth.*

Impact: Visionary outlook. Overall understanding of a leader's roles and responsibilities

Q54. *Imagine a situation where you have to deliver bad news to a colleague or client. How would you approach this conversation?*

Motive: Communication. Empathy. Maturity.

Answer: *Delivering bad news. whether professionally or on a personal level. requires sensitivity and clarity in communication. I would first choose a private setting for the conversation, and ensure I have all the necessary facts beforehand. I would then deliver the message directly and honestly, using an empathetic tone, with respect for the recipient's feelings and reaction. In case the news is work-related, I would also be prepared to answer questions and offer support or resources, if required. My goal would be to ensure the message is understood clearly, while minimizing any negative impact or reaction.*

Impact: Clear communication, with an empathetic approach and situational awareness.

Q55. *Thank you for your time today. Is there anything you'd like to ask us?* (Time to turn the tables, and leave that lasting impact that will be felt long after you have left the room!)

Motive: Career priorities. Maturity. Futuristic mindset.

Answer: *Thank you for taking the time to interview me today. I have three brief questions that I would like to ask. First, are there any specific work areas or tasks in this role that you would recommend me to focus on during the first month of employment? Second, what does the career progression path look like for this role? And finally, in your opinion, which skills and competencies are most critical for success in this position? I would greatly appreciate your insights and feedback, to help me mentally prepare for taking up this responsibility. Thank you.*

Impact: Posing these thoughtful parting questions will leave a lasting impression, positioning you as a candidate with clarity of purpose, one who is not only focused but already envisioning themselves thriving in the role. While no outcome is ever guaranteed, this final act of engagement could very well tip the scales in your favor, influencing the interviewer's decision positively.

Conclusion

As we conclude this book, it's evident that excelling in job interviews demands more than conventional preparation. By delving into these 55 unconventional questions and their answers, you've acquired crucial insights into how to distinguish yourself in any interview setting. Each question is designed to challenge norms and reveal your authentic capabilities, while the *'Motive'* and *'Impact'* briefs offer a deeper grasp of their strategic importance.

Embrace the challenges posed by unconventional questions as an opportunity to highlight your strengths and perspectives. With thorough preparation and a proactive mindset, you'll be well-equipped to excel in interviews and seize the opportunities that await. Apply these insights diligently; your readiness will set you apart and pave the way to your career success.

Remember, mastering these unconventional questions goes beyond having the right responses; it involves developing agility, your critical thinking, adaptability and communication skills. Continued practice and enhancement of these abilities will not only bolster your confidence, but also sharpen your competitive edge in the long run.

Thank you for exploring these unconventional interview strategies. Continue to push boundaries, and let your preparation be the catalyst for achieving new career milestones.

About the Author

Building on the success of my first book, *Find the Ladder*, acclaimed by corporate professionals, authors and career coaches, and honored with the 'Golden Book Award' from Literary Titan (USA) within three months of its publication, I leverage my extensive experience in career counseling and interview preparation.

With over four decades of perseverance and risk-taking in my career journey, I have guided countless professionals. I am excited to share new insights about interview preparation in this book, including a brief historical background on the origins of interviews, alongside innovative tips and perspectives, to help you excel in your next interview.

This work is dedicated to empowering job candidates, and providing recruiters with innovative interview questions to identify exceptional talent.

I remain committed to inspiring, guiding, and supporting individuals in their professional pursuits.

Find The Ladder on Amazon:

Follow my resources and connect with me, for ongoing career tips and guidance, and to attend my online and UAE-based career workshops.

My YouTube channel (dedicated to job-search and interview-prep assistance):

https://www.youtube.com/@nadeemlutfullah

Personal website (be the CEO of your career!):

https://www.thecareerceo.com

LinkedIn profile:

https://www.linkedin.com/in/nadeem-lutfullah

P.S. ...

I would sincerely appreciate it if you could take a moment to leave a brief, honest review on the platform where you purchased this book. Your insights are invaluable to me as an author, and will assist fellow readers in making informed choices. Thank you for your time and support.

Nadeem.

www.ingramcontent.com/pod-product-compliance
Lightning Source LLC
LaVergne TN
LVHW092054060526
838201LV00047B/1391